Fly to My Beginning

Fly to My Beginning

ARABELLA STELL

Foreword by Sian Gronlie

RESOURCE *Publications* · Eugene, Oregon

FLY TO MY BEGINNING

Resource Publications
An Imprint of Wipf and Stock Publishers
199 W. 8th Ave., Suite 3
Eugene, OR 97401

www.wipfandstock.com

PAPERBACK ISBN: 979-8-3852-5406-4
HARDCOVER ISBN: 979-8-3852-5407-1
EBOOK ISBN: 979-8-3852-5408-8

05/29/25

Foreword

I AM HONOURED TO write this foreword to a truly remarkable debut by the young Oxford-born poet, Arabella Stell. At just eight years old, Arabella presents a collection of poetry that is wholly original in voice and vision. These poems possess a rare magic—the power to refresh our perception of the world and of language itself. Her images can startle, but never jar; they surprise us with their clarity, insight, and emotional resonance.

Familiar words—*roses, darkness, birds, suns, stars*—are reborn in Arabella's hands, washed clean of cliché and made to shimmer with unexpected brightness. Her worldview is both innocent and wise, expressed in a style that moves effortlessly between simplicity and sophistication.

The 121 poems gathered here were written during Arabella's early years, yet they resist any attempt to categorise them as mere "children's poetry." They carry the depth and quiet authority of someone in tune with something much older than time. Her verses are infused with spiritual insight and prophetic intensity— echoing cycles of creation, destruction, and rebirth. In lines such as *"I gaze back to darkness, I choose to walk to my death"* and *"I fly out to my beginning,"* we glimpse a soul speaking from a place of fearless freedom, reminiscent of the mystical voice of Rumi in his poem *When I Die.*

Under the spell of Arabella's poetry, one begins to sense that her words rise from a timeless source—the same deep well from which all great poets draw. This collection is not just the beginning of a poetic journey; it is the arrival of a voice already attuned to the eternal.

In an age overshadowed by rapidly advancing technology, many fear that religion, art, and literature are fading into the glory of the past, as artificial intelligence begins to occupy the realms of both productivity and creativity. Yet this collection by Arabella Stell compels us to think otherwise. Her originality, depth, and imaginative power speak eloquently on behalf of a rising generation—one that is innately creative and unafraid to meet the complexity of the world into which they have been born. Arabella's poetry is a luminous reminder that the human spirit still burns brightly, and that the future of art is far from lost.

DR SIAN GRONLIE
Associate professor of Medieval Literature and Kate Elmore Fellow in English, St Anne's College, Oxford University
Oxford, January 2025

1

In the sky
I fly
Through jagged rocks
and high mountains
to the valley of music
where a thousand voices sing
a thousand orchestral music play
seven French horns ring out from low to high
two drums pound with all their might
clashing the clouds with lightening
Above the sound of rustling trees on the hilltops
I drowned
by the sound of music

2

Silence is in me
The flowing waters of peace takes my feet
I fall
I drop
Passed I go
to the valley of growth
into the stream
A voice howls
"turn back, turn back!"
I shudder, "A well of silence, peace be to you."
I looked up and fell flat on my face
On the shore of sleep, I stopped
"Who are you?" Cried, a mighty voice
I looked up but saw nothing except the night sky
I looked
and something suddenly blocked the view of the well of silence
Silence is but me

3

I walked to the shore
My feet sounded soften to nothing
The stars twinkled above and the tree sank into distance
A line of natural blue was spreading upon the shore
An upper line of blue was spreading on the horizon
thickening at every step
Which way?
I looked forward
There was nothing
but the calm sea

4

At each stroke of the boat
The sea moves
Through countless deserts
Numerous mountains
I follow the sea's rippling
I sink
At last, exhausted
into the gentle arms of the rocking sea
Awake
on an island
I wander about the isle
where at last, I find my home

5

In the air
Bird follow it
In the sea
Fish follow it
In the earth
Worms follow it
In the fire
Fire burns it
In an invisible place
It is received

6

In the air
A tiger stamps his feet
But how?
On the ground
It flies
In the sea
It lives
In the fire
It drowns
Under the earth
It is lost
But how?

7

In the sky
The bird who whistled the beginning of sunset has arrived
In the sea
There is only one type of fish
It has a halo on its head
But one big and mighty
On its back was a sentence written in the language of the Lord
This great fish waved its tail to twelve other fishes
They had each a word on their back but only one
Twelve more fish passed by
But on their heads, the halo had two different colours
Red was at the back and gold in the front
They followed a fish whose halo was pure gold
On his fin was a signature ring

8

In the air

The nightingale whistles the beginning of sunset through the branches of a tree

High on the hilltop

With the sun above, it was truly a sad site

For the sun looked down upon earth in a funeral state

The whistling died away and a silence came

That was unbearable to be with

The clouds faded away

leaving a solemn landscape

The stars looked down in despair at the dreary landscape that lay beneath them

The moon itself looked dismayed

as it saw the deserted world

once full of happiness

peace

joy

and laughter

had shrunk

into a place of sadness

chaos

despair

and

silence

With a shudder, the earth exploded

But away in the east
a new star
stretched itself

9

In the air
A swallow flies
High mountains, ice caves, jungle forest
and hornets' nests
Far out beyond the mortal realm
to the peaceful valley
In the lake, fishes swim
They never go beyond the lake
for fear of the raging ocean
In the sea
a dolphin swims
high coral beds
dangerous sea valleys
kale forests
and sharks lair far beyond the sea creatures' realm
To the upper forms of valleys
In the beautiful sky, birds fly upward
They never go beyond for fear of the weather

10

In the shallow lake

Lies a crocodile with a silly grin on its long face

Shoals of fish floke together in the evening when the crocodile
lies asleep

The flowers are blossoming and the bigger they are the more
beautiful

Sheep floke here together in the morning, when the flowers are
asleep

In the forest, the trees grow tall and laden with fruit in the spring

Bugs crowed here in winter when the trees are asleep

In the lake bed, dead fish are often found

Tadpoles come here to eat the flesh of the dead fish

On the flower stems different bugs feast, they being green are
hidden securely

When they feed, ants come to check which one is producing
liquid

Inside of a tree, ants floke, red, black, brown

Trees, lakes, meadows, all form the valley of peace

1 1

In the world you are nothing than dust
The world is all around you
Walk
gaze
and
drink
the wonder
of the
universal space

12

The star shines down upon me
As I walk through the forest of emerald green
Far away but getting closer at each step is a calm line of blue
across the horizon
Quite slowly, the ground softened at each step and every step
quietened
As I walk, I gaze upon the moon which seems to shine like the
stars
It passes by
shining brightly
so, the sea turns sapphire blue
As I wander
a glorious site appears
Two dolphins stood nose to nose in the sea
I run towards them
and they scoop me out of the sea
Home
Moon!

13

In the sky, clouds are turning westward
Sandy desert
icy caves
into the abyss
Far above, a wren sings
Clouds are missed
With nothing to hide
both the sun and the moon
day and night
is always around
No sleep
until someone
dares to go into the abyss

14

In the air
nature whistled a song of happiness
Echoing afar
the sun stretched its rays to listen
In the raging ocean, the stem lies
The stem grew tall
beneath the ocean's depth
And
shone a summer's time of light
towards the coast

15

In the sky
the sun used to shine
started to fade away into darkness
Away in the west
destruction prepared to destroy the earth

16

In the sky
the swallow flies
until with aching wings
he stopped at the gate of hell
Before the gate
a crow
and a raven stood
The crow looked up
and a flash of anger ran crosses his face
The swallow pleaded for entrance
but not a bit would the raven stir

17

In the sky
the world fade away
through distance lands
Time goes by
Through distance land
a river flows
In Octopus arms
the world is far
Through distance land, I fly
to the world of peace
Joy

18

The stars
shine down upon me
I walk to my death
floating in a stream
At last
peace arrives

19

In fire
I shoot out like water and fire combined in the wildness
Stars shone through the window like branches
Sky whistles far above me
the clearing across the woods are unbearably bright
Through distance glimpses
a land
full and new
had appeared
Through grass
tulips
insets
buzzing bees
worm holes
caterpillars
and silver beds
autumn feasts
travelling in time
a frost of colours
with sorrow
passing the sun's pitiful face
but
a cheerful smile
on the face of wild wind

Winter always come too soon
Clashing clouds
and whirling wheat, barley
hungry grass, cold trees and shivering fields
Icy mountains and peaceful animals, hibernating in cold weather
Sleeping bees in their nest
icy caves and freezing chill
Winter warmth and fiery lair
out of winter into spring!

Things growing
harvest working
Through the cloud
wind bellows away in defeat
while the sun beams proudly
but gently upon the face of earth
So bright
it shone hedgehogs, bees, dormouse
and other hibernating animals came out
dance to the music of sun beams
Rain
fell gently
upon the thirsty grass
until the earth full, cried out to the rain "give me no more for I
am well satisfied."
The rain
with a sigh fell one last time only to vanish into distance
A colourful substance, skipped into view
Rainbow at last came into sight
clouds started to dress her in white

so bright colours of her own shining like the sun
It danced, gently splashing its colour
When the time was right
A sun went up
up through the clouds
a joyful cry went, "summer is here!"
Then, I heard the sound of orchestra notes sprang up
In the valley of music
distance melodies
and faraway tones
a thousand voices sing
from
inside
of the earth

2 0

At first
there was no light
But something shone in the left horizon
Light fell onto darkness
and the universe lifted up
But no light as beautiful as the divine light
which shone before the beginning

Plain, bare and neatly made
it rose into existence
Then a liquid substance began to flow
covering the world with blue
Rising above it
a dome shaped sky covers the waters
It was the same colours as the waters
When arising
it was a dome shaped
but not when it stopped arising
Blue light and airy, twirled around in the grace of its skirt

2 1

I stand in summer
the cool breeze pours around me
I stand on the shore
the stars loyally look down unto me
Waves gently wash my feet
clean I go into heaven
The guardian of the gate awaits me
There are twelve gates
and twelve cities you must pass through, he said softly to me
I went through the first, the city of music
The roofs were of wood, bricked walls were of gold
Amid all the buildings, stood a temple, high and erect
From inside, I heard a thousand instruments play
I stepped inside
every brick was gold
but no material inside of the temple
could match the instrument's dazzling beauty
As soon as I stepped out
I saw a portal with no guardian angel except a letter
When I got to the next
I saw everything the same
but the entire house was made of a song
I went through ten more to the holy throne

22

Emerald green grass
sway to the music of shaking trees
Fair the sun shines upon rubious rosebuds
Clouds gently fade
in the sky a rainbow doth appear
Sweet the Rainbow looks upon the world of flowing sunshine
The sun looks gently down upon the waves on silent beach
Sky spread high above
spreading its blue wings across the light field universe
Evening draws down the day into a beautiful ending
stars gently appear
The moon looks back at the sun
who gently fades away into a cloud of sable black
The stars
who are lost souls
wondering in the darkness
The moon
shines with all its possible light upon the sleeping world
The sun
reclining on a cloud of darkness
looks solemnity down upon the eerie darkness
Away in the west
destruction prepares itself

23

Clashing clouds
whirling storms
away the strange bird went
Sharp mountains
high hills
and stormy deserts
until
at last
he started complaining, "why did I go travelling?" he mourned
Away he went
until
with exhaustion
aching wings he landed on a snowy mountain
Over and across was a brook
So, swooping he went
Suddenly
he was back
to his old self

24

That day
did the sun shine
did the spider weave
but like the star
that glows in the east
does destruction prepare itself in the west
where would the star illuminate
if sun and moon
stayed
but wavered not
over the molten ground
golden tears
went down
to
the light

25

Oh, behold the golden rain
that was once flowing
flew down
like flames coming from the eternal flame
Grasses swept down
ever before in an array of light
and away doth the angels sing
Oh, in vain
did the trees bow
to alcoves glorious array
but none did it say
its trees grew tall in swamps
but swayed in the pain
alcove boughs bent
to weeping grass
but the leaves refused to fall

26

In the sky
earth gives light to us
In the air
sun fools us
In the clouds
moon gives us imagination
Stars
make us think
The whole universe
is huge
but we
are nothing
more than
dust
in a field of movement

27

The last flame that lit the earth
fell on the earth
Upon a snowy branch
a caterpillar crawled into a tree
Autumn bees sang in different melodies
Snakes came out of their burrows
The flame struck
it lit the earth up like a star
but earth's creatures were full of hope

28

In autumn feast
winter comes
Harsh times in snowy dell
to winter forests and cold well
Mighty lakes to frozen ice
Streaming patterns
whirling stream
form a thunderstorm against the window pane
Thunder
Thunder
I hear no sound
Safe in a bed I go
Crash!

29

On the riverbed
sun danced with fish
In her bright rainment
she danced along the riverbed
slashing its lioness mane
So bright did she dance
the moon was dazzled by her rays
Filled with rage
he went to her
and challenged her to see whether she could send somebody to
sleep
But he never won
for his rays were not bright enough

30

In the universe
we are nothing
but stars in the sky
Dust is soil
soil is dust
So far away
another lay
Denser than fire
the oort cloud lay
Pleiades shining glimmering in the west
The moon fades
let the sun rises
To the open moon
every dent is like having a cut
which looks like a dent in cream
The sun twirling her golden mane
tosses her head to the pleading moon

3 1

In the sky
a golden shape was made
It had a great shift
which shimmered in the sky
Though it shone
There was no decoration
except for a few rays of fire
These rays could be seen from a long distance
Away in the west
stood a planet so vast it was
but too small to overpower the sun
On the earth
grew trees
vegetables
grass
and there were oceans
animals
fish
and plants

32

Still an angel from afar
gone to exile in barren land
In hunting lakes
does it feed
Camels stray to a distance path
For fish swim in lakes of glee
be eaten before
Worlds end

33

Through sky I dream to stars
I walk on rainbow
I wade into shallow water
l crash down to a valley
I fly out to my beginning

34

A nightingale flies
over
chilling night
over
to the clouds
but none
does winter
spear

35

In the sky
earth fades away
into clouds through distant lands
Time passes
through rainbows I fly
Stars turn away from me
I gaze back to darkness
I chose to walk to my death

36

In fire
eyes gaze out like stars
The sun shines through trees in the sky
leaves whistle above me
The clearing of forest
awakes me
to hear the sound of dogs barking away

37

Cold trees
shivering hills
and mountains
desolation islands drifted away
in the wind

38

The sound of music echoed from afar
instruments play joyfully in the sky
In the valley of orchestra
melodies flow from afar
a thousand voices sing from under the earth
The whale leapt high
a splash of music occurred from beneath the sea
The valley of music both up and down
flowed through clouds
of sunset
and sunrise

39

I dance
above the mountains
of the west
I fly
with the moon
I fly
in the sea
I fly
through the mountain's eye
to see clearly
the morning star shine
in
the Eastern sky

40

Wind blew me off the mountain cliff
I hung on the cliff
Yet the wind swept me away into the darkness
I walked in the west
Yet I still cling on to the cliff's eastern face

41

A shadow
passes by
as I stand in the sand
My soul
sinks into the darkness
I turn back
into the wild
as I look down
upon the sand

42

A horse stamped by
as I bathed in a near spring
I followed it into a lake
I stepped into a pool
that pool
was of melted silver

43

The rose blossomed
in the summer's morning
It glowed
in the morning rise
The rose
grew strong under her care
but she was old
weak
and frail
in her old age

44

The horse took care of me
Under its fruitful care
the mountains shone bright just like I
The horse went
into the earth
until dawn

45

The sky
looked upon the moon
and from afar
the sun grew weary of holding up her shimmering rays
The last weak beam of life
fell through the moon to the earth
The beam
broke out
into darkness

46

A rose
once loved the sun
but the rose
was dazzlled
by its shining ray
Yet
a sunflower
was wise to disobey the rose
and hid in the sunset of trees
In the west
Rose died
in the heat
of the sun

47

Stars
are talking gold
in night sky
Moon
is a great song of silver
that hung up
on the line
of melodies

48

I walk
in the west
I talk
with disruption
I sweep
through pity
I whisper
to the moon
I shimmer
in the sunlight
I dance
with the stars

49

I am
but a star in the air
I fall
through the wind
I think
through time

50

In the tree

a screech owl hides

Waiting for the time to shriek joyfully the destruction of the world

At last

Freeing itself from the crack

It flew away

51

A wild oak
lived in the woods
Many trees were planted
in the pleasant mountains
but
none stretched out
as far as the wild oak

52

Upon
the angelic surface
of gold
a star
shines

53

There is
nothing
but
the lives
in a jar
colours
shine
from afar

54

In the fairest love the world
Swims a heart shape
Sun polishes its surface
Moon in its short head
looked away into the lles of love

55

In the air
cloud wonder and ponder if birds have wings
grass wonder and ponder if tiger have legs
Over the bare fields
flame ingates the rocky valley
and sets it in flame
The bird swoops low
and flies down onto the angelic surface of gold
The fire
burned a great hole in the sky
Suddenly
a flood rushed down upon the earth

56

I faded away from the beginning
I am it
I wondered
if you were a star
born in the sky
I dreamt abroad
into lles of numbers
Yet
I forgot about it

57

Oh, did the winter harken unto me
that spring hath come
I did not have a word
utter the winter's proof of delight
I stepped up
upon the fire
and from the ash
an angel ascended
into the sunset

58

I dance
through song
I swim
in melodies
l walk
into music's caring dell
l light up
like a star
I look behind me at the closing gate
Death is approaching in the morning
Yet
I could run faster than a deer
I trip

59

The nightingale
sang a song of war
and strife
Her skill
enchanted those
who sought her for miserable reasons
Thy wing's strength
is the like of the wind
howling through the storm

60

Wind
grew strong
and
in a fit of rage
blew its mother away

61

I walk
in valley's stream
I skate
on ice
The hissing sound
of music
reached my ears

62

The waves
shone through
the horses' mane
The shining mane
of crystal gold
shone
in the fading sunlight

63

The stars
looked down
upon the lowly ground
while
the sun
moved away
in sleep

64

The grass
went down
into the stream
while the shepherd
grazed its sheep
The mill
in the tower
wove long strands of blue
curling down the trees
and holding up
the sun dusts

65

Oh, thou art like a baying mare
therefore
you toss yourself
to pleading suit
yet
you are
like the blossoming cherry trees
dainty
in all their ways

66

Wend thine own ways
oh birds of the wild
wither dost thou go
wend thine own ways
oh me of the earth
flew into
the clouds of dawn

67

They are around me
They shine in the morning
where I sit down
in summer's early glow
morning fades into noon
As it turned into evening
the sky turned to night
Dawn wept
on the face of the earth

68

A flash of blue ran
August flew by
in the wavering dawn

69

Stars

flew above sea

Moon

vanished from earth

Sun

hid behind those drawing clouds

Clouds turned west

to the sun

where morning drew near

The world grew still

under cold weather

beneath moon

animals

frozen

and all forgot about the flame of hope

Stars

streaked down upon the sand

The world

shone through its own dell

Stars

went their ways

into their starry dell

Their light

disappeared from the sun

Stars

drew near upon the ever-ending reign

The star
looks down upon the enchanting stream of moonlight
and made a bridge of flames
in the starry mountains
In earth's ancient dell
the flame goes

70

The bridge of flame
dug deep
into the ground
The sky
shone bright in the evening stars
The wind howling grew louder
but the hedgehog
was unaware
of the ever-wailing sound

71

The soil shook
and cracked down
into the darkness
of the black hole
The world
lit up
in flames
and in despair
the world shrank down
to a very high end

72

The large world pierced out
into many millions of fragments
The world grew dim
under the ever-wishing sunlight
The sun shrank away
in its deepest regret

73

Lo, doth the clouds morn over the moon
yet I frail not a word of my heart
The sword pierces my wretched soul
yet I make no sound to my death

74

Thou art
but as sweet as a rose
Colours thy self
like this dasmak rose
The sun
shines fair
over the fading dasmak rose

75

Gallop thy horse wen the battle ends
Smoothen thy crest of brided brown
Near the end
a bloody rose of blessed triumph reign
The general in grizzled armour
looked upon the rose
Right to the left
would be a bodkin
curtle
falcon
poniard
rapier
partisan
and pike

76

Men
walked away
to the campus
in clocked garbidans
mantals
or frocks
Clothed in winter
the fires

77

Thou art
as sweet as a garden of rubious roses
The sun
looks down upon the pied field
The dasmask horse
eat in faraway fields
Dun coloured cows
sleep in a sleeping world

78

Thou art
like lilies in a pond
White lilies turned
by sending a sound
like a thousand oboes
lutes
and wid-de-gambols

79

The ounce lept away
as the soldiers shot
A cocktress swept low
and devoured a cough
A gib crept by
and devoured a martlet
A howlet flew by
Apard crept
attracting many fishes
A paddock swam
for a second
before diving
into the unknown

80

The shallow water
reflects the moon's hoary face
The constellation Leo
Pisces
and Virgo
looked down
from the sky

81

Ladies in their saffron frocks dance by
Over words do they cross over to the creator's name
Gentlemen with their heads held up
get parted ways from their wives
by the turning page

82

My soul is the like of a lion
Stars are nothing but lost souls
Darkness of the night is only a wave of inky black
Moon itself is but a grizzled rock in space
The land beyond land
is the like of a dimensional space

83

Oh thou art like a baying mare
therefore
you toss your head to suitor's plea
yet
you are as sweet as cherry blossom
wafting down the breeze
dainty
in all thy ways

84

Oh leaf
thine own family branches far up
Clean thy way to hard life
Be rotten
or eaten
or swept away
into the river
Oh
little leaf

85

Thou art
like the baying mare
The cool autumn breezes
shares thy fragrance
Flowing hair
ripples through the breeze
Clothed
in dasmask and roses
dance
to the music
of
the swaying trees

86

Oh
thou angels
wen it is at end
grant they holy land peace forevermore
Yom Kippour wen thou art at rest
grace thy wings to the holy soil
Bless Israel
and wen the holy land is done
the Messiah will come

87

I am

like a swan

on a lake

The stars

shine down

in a thousand hues

yet

they shine dimly

A storm

is to come

Rain

pours overhead

The gate of heaven is opening

yet

no mortal knows that

an angel is pouring water

from a watering can

Suddenly

the bolt of heavenly light escaped down to earth

It came from the gate of sadness

The miserable ones far above

threw torches far ahead

88

Oh
thine footsteps
are the like of those of calves
Oh
thine shimmering fur
of thy days
Come higher and rest in thy days
Rest
Eat
Forevermore

89

The tree cried
"wind! Rain! Thee!"
before it fell
After the storm
leaves
glistening
on many trees

90

Through foreign lands
a world of youth and flowers
A flowering world shine ahead
A world of happiness clouds the mind
A small speck of joy glisten
In the sky of eyes
an empty throne

91

Storm is howling
The sun looks on
Trees and bushes
are blown away into darkness
Wild West
So huge is the storm
how small is earth

9 2

The three baby angels
in my room
often crept by me
Their skins
were of a hidden hue
Their wings
were colours of chestnut brown and dark green
Their eyes
were of dark brown
and Tibetan blue

93

This world
shone bright
under the Sun
While our moon
faded away
The light
span
throughout the world
I see clearly
Every dust
in unique dresses
twirling out from darkness
one
by
one

94

Still I am
not a word dost thou speak of thou self
You take my spawn yet ponder not
Am I as clear as you hath said the rose devoured the donkey
Thy horse

95

The song
flew over stream
into willow tree
The stream
swept a song
into waters
Many grasses
slipped themselves
into stream
Thin weeds of yellow dawn
flew out into earth
Afar the radiant sun
skipped
skipped away
into darkness

96

Radiant stars
made the first starlight go into view
the sky fell down like a flower
Still alone in sky
the world weakened
deep into the surface

97

The saffron sun
ran through the world
Twilight went around trees
Though on land
clouds
reached down
they did not reach over mountains
Into twilight by storm
winds gathered themselves
out of the twilight

98

Echo
wandered off
into horizon
A lowly warmth
gathered into a hope
Moon
echoed
by the winter dawn
Winter
dawned
onto the autumn
yet
afar the battle in the world
ceased to a new beginning

99

The song
flew out
from the seasons
to the stream
where grasses
swept themselves
into the waterfall
The willow
pushed away leaves
from their homes
into the faraway distance
New shoots
grew out of the wildness
The frail willow
accepted flowers
into its last caring sigh

100

So much
like a flower
in autumn's dread
a star
would fly out to its beginning
but the flower
would not
more like the star
it would mourn
for its life
unaware this simple dread could come too soon
Life for life it lay
awaiting the call of spring
but winter appeared
In a sorrow
This flower's pedal dropped one and one
unto the soil
spreading in winter's chilling call
A bird saddened
by watching
It had to fly for a country with warmth
where stars born again and again
And ignoring the flower's very sad fate

101

In winter's fading cry
earthly flowers growing
In growing abundance
the call flies
to winter's cold abode
Melting it to water's ash
Trees opened their eyes
suddenly taller than before

In spring's early call
A storm went to the land of storms
where they lived
Making no sound
lest rain will come
But rain still fell to the ground
As the sun has quickly moved away
to not display her shining rays

102

One last time did the sun shine
One last time did the earth smile
One last time did the moon glimmer
One last time did waves move
One last time did the ground shake
One last death moved a tear
One last action moved a soul
One last sigh moved a heart
One last soul was in movement
One last time the star wept aloud
One last time a soul went through time
One last time the angel sang
One last time the bird fell
One last war went to peace
One last death did I cry
One last time I shared my hope
One last time I fly to my beginning

103

In silence
river flows
In peace
bird flies
In dread
animal walks
Outside time
angel sits
Through time
devil walks
In dread
the stream flows not
In pity
the stream will not flow
In sunlight bird have wings
In haste demon hide

104

I fly
over the valley
I fly
across the valley of peace
Yet
alone
It is perilous fly over the stream
but over I go
to the valley of perilous path
I journey through forests after forest
Through barren desert after barren desert
to meet
the jaws of the snake

105

In breaking dawn
I often fly
through those dreams of mine last night
Does the wings of my mind
take me to where I go
or my wings take my mind on a fly
I know not
But through the stream of thoughts
I often fly
to the sea
Yet
I do not stop anywhere
I fly higher than the seagulls
I fly lower than the earth
I fly through dream to reality
I fly through reality to dream
I often fly

106

In fire
a radiant light
Inside
a beast's eye glowing like death growing
In shallow water
a forgotten secret lies
never to be discovered
Far beyond the mountain passage
a lion's den awaits
forever awaits

107

So much more than a star
but less than wild wind passes
Far away in distance
but less than an angel
yet
not too much
not too less
just fine
for me

Higher above the clouds
Lower beneath the sea
Yet
not too low
not too high
just right
for me

108

Vast oceans in countless places
Yet I know not of where they came
All the sea shells are old
and have no beginning
My mind search through
Books of old
Yet as I look
The pages have no end

109

Through this world
decades and decades go by
I know not how to count them
But watch
millions of time flying away
One after another
They all came to an end
Yet
some of their substance remain

110

Silent

yet alone

does the wind lower her pride

So do I remain

Haunting forests hinder me not

I walk deeper into the unknown

Silent

and subtle

does the wind lower her pride

111

In the sky
The bird would have flown, had not the animals come to view
But more alike were the bird that was sent to the sky
Different were the animals on land who knew each other
The bird
So fast like the wind
So clear as sky's night
So farther than the morn
So more than the trees
More glorious than light
More pitiful than sunlight
Yet open in all words
All greater than animals of land
Yet
There are places
Greater than animals of the earth known
far beyond places the bird have explored

1 1 2

The silence in a pond drifts into thin air
While the ending of moon takes flight
Wind pours itself in fury
as the sun takes its place
Rain runs for his life
as the longer he stays
the more it burns his eye
And in his anger
he held up in the storm's palace
listening to the songs of nature
only frustrated
On the surface of stilled pond
waves of melodies
passing through

113

Twilight comes as the sun fades
patiently it waits for the ghosts to come out
of the graveyard
But to the bird's dismay
They turned and fled

114

Waterfall bent its head to time
Yet time increased his fatal silence
The waterfall pleaded in vain
But time ignored the passing years
Slowly did the waterfall that give up on life
Birds on seeing the waterfall dead
Sang away in sorrow

115

In the pond the fishes
grow golden scales
but one would
grow no more
as the sun burned the fish's back
He decided to swim through darkness
Daring to make sound as he slid away quietly
Groping his way to the moon
Leaving the sun behind

116

The land grows strong in forever rest
but through winter it dies
As twilight arose
dawn faded
Saddened were the plants
In muddy streams it withered
that they elapsed into eternal sleep

117

Through wailing forest
wind howls
Through eternal light
The path of holy light appears
Across the cage of guilt
into the lost wild
enter the fire of incarnation

118

My soul drifts into the unknown
allow spirit leads to destiny
Truth flies and twinkles in space
Those who sing see angels
Those who seek knowledge lead to the past
An endless circle draws

119

In the sullen ground

A new seed came to life

but none would hear its calling

120

Silent is the waterfall

that flows through earth

Watching torment grief and pain

Its soul flew down to heaven with a song

where angels flipping wings

Yet none heard the pleading song of the waterfall

Its water graduate gone dry

Though none saw it die

It stayed in piles of white ash

Its song wavered

until

at last

it lay to rest

in the air

1 2 1

In the depth of willows
The song refused to sing
This gloomy silence
has caused countless flowers on the ground to wither
waited for long
As the song would not sing
A golden willow with fewer branches
started to sing in a small voice
Its eco from afar was even louder
Yet it was not the song's own melody
Nor the melody of choir of angels
But it continued for days

www.ingramcontent.com/pod-product-compliance
Lightning Source LLC
LaVergne TN
LVHW051132080426
835510LV00018B/2373